A COLLECTION OF WORDS

A COLLECTION OF WORDS Copyright © 2020 by Art of Telling Publications, LLC. All rights reserved. No part of this publication may be used or reproduced in any manner whatsoever without written permission except in the case of brief quotations embodied in critical articles and reviews. For information address Art of Telling Publications, P.O. Box 312, Hazlet, NJ 07730

Library of Congress Control Number 2020906098

ISBN 978-1-7348447-0-2

10 9 8 7 6 5 4 3 2 1

*Dedicated to the words of men and women everywhere—
transcribed, transduced, repurposed, and deeply felt.*

*And to time, merciless time, as it goes on and on and allows
matters of this world to be born, grow, and die.*

Also by Sea Gudinski:

1969: A BRIEF AND BEAUTIFUL TRIP BACK

A
COLLECTION OF
WORDS

THE WRITINGS OF
SEA GUDINSKI

CONTENTS

<u>POETRY</u>

A COLLECTION OF WORDS	17
WORDS AND THEIR WORTH	18
THESE WORDS ARE IN TECHNICOLOR	21
A SIMPLE TRUTH	23
HISTORY REPEATS…	24
EGO & PREJUDICE	25
THE FEAR	27
ROCK-A-BYE-BABY	29
TIME	33
IF	35
?	37
REFLECTIONS	39
DREAMING OF NIRVANA	40
SYNCH	42
THE LOOKING GLASS	44
WEATHER-MAN	47
THE WINDOW	48

THE SEVEN DEADLY SINS	49
THE POSTER	50
SO'HAM ASMI, UNUS MUNDUS	51
BEN	52
THE MUSIC SHOPPE	53
PLAY ME SOMETHING BLUE	55
ANOTHER SHORT POEM ABOUT WORDS	56
OLD STOMPING GROUNDS	57
SOME NIGHTS	58
LOVE IS	59
YOU HAVEN'T LOVED…	61
A WOMAN WALKED INTO THE OCEAN	62
THE LIGHT	64

PROSE

PROMETHEUS' FOLLY	69
THE MIRROR	71
COEXIST	74
NIGHT TERRORS	76
A CURT RANT ABOUT THE EVILS OF THE WORLD	79
ESOTERIC MUSINGS OF A DAY LABORER	82
THE SEA	85
A MUSING	86
MADNESS	87
A CONTEMPLATION	88
_____	89
THE POSSIBLE IMPOSSIBILITY	91

A COLLECTION OF WORDS

POETRY

A COLLECTION OF WORDS

All literary works are simply a collection of words:

Intended to make you feel something

                —or not.

Intended to make you see something

                —or not.

Intended to make you understand something

                —or not.

Intended to make you be something

                —or not.

Intended to make you experience something

                —always.

WORDS AND THEIR WORTH

What is it about words that we find so irresistibly alluring?

Is it their strange yet mystifying capacity to be combined
                                    deconstructed
                    worn away into obscurity
                    and created anew
the reason we find them so fascinating?

—That we as a race should build for them temples and shrines and grant their writers immortality?

What is the distinction between a cluster of words and a string of words?

What is the influence of words dictated
                                    whispered
                                          written
                                              orated
                                        passive
                                    active
                            descriptive?

Is it all purely relative?

Wherein do they derive their power? Their potential for enlightenment
            destruction
                    expression
                          explanation
                                beauty?

WORDS AND THEIR WORTH

What is the grammatical difference between the truth and a lie?

Is it the denotation?
                Connotation?
                        Suffix?
                              Prefix?
                                    Root?
The antecedent or the subject-verb agreement?

Bare-bones brittle words—sticks and crosses
                            slopes and dots
                                barks and growls
                                    whines and moans.

—Is there a single, definable divide between the beauty and value inherent in a poet's missives and the indeterminable jabber of a homeless schizophrenic?

Between a graduate student's dissertation and your bibulous babbling when you've had a few too many?

Between *Ulysses* and *Jabberwocky*?

Between the untranslated *Canterbury Tales* and last century's *Finnegan's Wake?*

What must be done to words in order for them to henceforth accrue value?

Must they be made to sing?
                            To dance?

WORDS AND THEIR WORTH

> What gives these meaningless strokes of a pen,
> contractions of the vocal cords such scintillating life?
>
> This rhetoric finds conclusion and respite in subjectivity
>
> ::::: All these answers are simply up to you.

THESE WORDS ARE IN TECHNICOLOR

These words are blue...

as blue as the crying eyes that fall upon them
as blue as the broken heart that gives them life
as blue as the realm from which they come.

These words are red...

as red as the lips that speak them
as red as the passions that enflame them
as red as the blood that pours through the veins of you
                            and I who share through them.

These words are yellow...

as yellow as the daytime sun and the soft glow of lanterns
                            that illuminate them
as yellow as the aged pages upon which they are penned
as yellow as the road they take us down time and time
                                            again.

These words are black...

as black as the ink in which they are dressed
as black as the fears and secrets they expose
as black as the futility they embody, that hangs over the
                            human race like a cloud.

THESE WORDS ARE IN TECHNICOLOR

These words are white…

as white as the spaces that define them
as white as the enlightenment contained within them
as white as the miracle they are—that of making
                              thoughts and feelings tangible.

These words are in Technicolor…

    and through their versatility they are set to become

            a little something for everyone.

A SIMPLE TRUTH

In all the things you are
There is a little bit of me;
Because no matter how near or far,
We are all just one great big human family.

Yes, I know it sounds cliché,
But still I cannot buy
Why so many of us must every day
Go to war to fight and die.

No matter if you're black or white, yellow, tan, or blue;
Live in New York, Bangkok, Nice, or Islamabad;
Believe the world sits on a turtle or are an orthodox Jew;
Every last one of us is a child of God.

And maybe in ten to twenty thousand years
When the nuclear smoke begins to clear,
Another race will set foot on Earth and say:
Humans were a funny bunch, too bad they had no brains.

HISTORY REPEATS...

History repeats,

but only it's defeats.

You can rally

and you can tally.

You can fight

with all your might.

You can push and you can shove,

but really what is missing here is love.

The world may have turned,

but we really haven't learned.

EGO & PREJUDICE

That man over there looks different than me;
my friend he surely cannot be.
His skin is not the same and he wears different clothes,
how many other things are wrong only God knows.
This is my Ma and this is my Pa;
sure, they look different from me as well,
but there's certainly a resemblance, can't you tell?

That man over there talks different than me;
my friend he surely cannot be.
Arabic, German, Spanish, or Tamil—
it all sounds like gibberish still.
This is my daughter, born with a lisp;
sure, when she speaks she sounds different than me,
but I can still understand her, don't you see?

That man over there follows a different religion than me;
my friend he surely cannot be.
My faith is right, his is just a game,
don't you even try to tell me they're all the same.
This is my wife, her parents are of another sect;
but the difference in doctrine is really so minor,
and we share the same hopes to which we aspire.
Sure, in some ways they think differently than me,
but on all the important points we still agree.

EGO & PREJUDICE

That man over there promotes a different political
system than me;
my friend he surely cannot be.
He is an ignorant extremist, a senseless wingnut
who backs the wrong party and is the reason our country
is in a rut.
This is my brother, a moderate at heart;
sure, our thoughts on policy may collide,
but at least we're still on the same side.

THE FEAR

There is fear in people's eyes like never before—
when we turn on the news all we see is gore.
Depraved and violent is the human race—
corrupt, immoral sinners since our fall from grace.
We are afraid of the government we allow to rule us—
all those taxes, laws, and surveillance and we hardly make a fuss.
We are afraid the food we buy is made to kill—
it's really too bad we eat it still.
We are afraid our water is contaminated—
and if we drink it, we will soon be eradicated.
We are afraid indeed of the state of our land—
don't you know it's all been done by our hand?
We are afraid to live and afraid to die—
wouldn't it be something if we only asked why?
Those who believe are afraid of their God—
and he who does not is simply a clod.

THE FEAR

> We are afraid of the truth, only a few are wise—
>
> the rest of us just embrace the lies.
>
> We are afraid of each other and that's truly the worst—
>
> to hate one another, we must dislike ourselves first.
>
> We are pitted brother against brother—
>
> I wish we could understand we all share the same Mother.

ROCK-A-BYE-BABY

Rocking, rocking, rocking along…

Sweet little babe in my arms, right where you belong.

Go on to sleep now, if I should be so blessed;

I'll sing you a song, if only you'll rest.

I'll rock you 'til morning, if that is the key—

Come on little baby, close those wide blue eyes for me!

One of these days you'll be too big for me to hold,

Rocking in a pine-wood chair, curious and bold.

Oh little baby you'll grow up right and you'll grow up fine;

How proud you'll make me, how bright you'll shine!

A tall, handsome man with long dark hair

And a beautiful smile to show that you care.

No strong wind will rock you,

Nor will the deep ocean blue;

You'll go off one day as all little boys do.

It won't always be easy, it won't always be fun;

Sometimes you'll be sad when the day is done.

ROCK-A-BYE-BABY

I can't tell you how it makes me feel,

Knowing this is all too real.

The thought of you alone,

Out there in the world all on your own—

But when you come to say goodbye,

I'll rock you in a hug and cover my eyes so you won't see me cry.

There'll be heartbreak out on that long rocky road,

And you'll probably carry a big heavy load.

There'll be worries, uncertainty, and fear of defeat,

But I pray you'll press on and never retreat

Because the cake that you bake, you always get to eat.

Diligence and hard work are always awarded

And good intentions justly rewarded.

Though mistakes and surprises may rock your world,

Don't get discouraged, don't let your efforts become unfurled.

ROCK-A-BYE-BABY

I pray you'll have success and acclaim,

Joy and affluence and maybe even fame.

In all of your life I wish you peace of mind,

And time away from work on the grind.

If your thoughts are pure and your words are true,

All of these things will come to you.

I hope you find a woman who'll always treat you right,

One who'll hold you and rock you through the night.

And maybe one day you'll have a rock-a-bye-baby too—

Just like how once upon a time I rocked you.

I hope you grow old, much older than me.

Creased with laugh lines your face will be.

Seated in a chair whose rocking is slow,

Surrounded by a family whose love you know.

I suppose, no doubt, there will come a day,

And when it does, let it come as it may.

With love in your eyes and peace in your heart,

Off to heaven you'll surely depart.

ROCK-A-BYE-BABY

You'll feel the rocking of soft angels' wings,

The same as when Mama rocks you and sings.

In the future, there'll be plenty of time for these things,

But for now, my song is over, the day is at its end,

The sun has no more daylight to lend.

And for you, little baby, just go on to sleep.

From you I don't want to hear not even a peep.

When you wake up tomorrow, I'll be rocking you still;

I'd rock you forever, if that was God's will.

Sleep, little baby, Mama won't let you fall—

I'm just going to rock you, cradle and all.

TIME

Soon it will be April, May, June, and December.
Soon it will be my birthday, don't you remember?
Easter comes next and Christmas after that,
And then it will be time to turn the clocks back.
Summer comes on slow
As the leaves begin to grow;
And right after the Fourth,
Cool winds blow in from up north.
And just like that four years have passed,
Maybe now I'll have some time at last!

Or not, it seems
Time is the stuff of dreams.
September is here,
The weather is clear.
The kids are back in school,
And the nights turn cool.

And just like that they're graduating,
Isn't that intimidating?
I remember that picture like it was yesterday,
And when "twenty years ago" was something I couldn't say.

In no time at all it's winter again,
Time to say goodbye to my old friends.
Wouldn't you know my anniversary is here,
And I've been married for thirty-five years!

TIME

Now I'm getting invitations for reunions and showers,
And as my hands work away the hours,
Time just keeps ticking on and on.
Before long, I'll be gone.
Maybe one day I'll be back here once more;
I just wish I knew what it was all for.

IF

The future is that faceless sage;
> that nameless monster;
>> that escaping word on the tip of your tongue.

The future is eminent doom to those afeared and pie in the sky to amorous lovers.

The future is endless while the past is quick;
> kind yet merciless;
>> fanciful yet dim.

The future is alive and bright in the eyes of our children;
> yet it dies in each passing moment—
>> that momentous paradox—
> growing both longer and shorter with each second;
spinning its yarn freely in our dreams.

Dreams—the breath that gives life to uncertainty!

Nowhere else but in a man's mind can be found the
> incomparable allure of a dream,
> set in a time that may never come.

Whereas the destiny of the present is to die with time,
> the future lives forever—
>> it stands eternal in a mortal world.

IF

Every man is born with a future,
>   but few acknowledge a past—
>   > without which no future could exist.

While the past is the devil's playground,
>   and the present is man's decision,
>   > the future is the realm of God.

It is omniscient;
>   omnipresent;
>   > and most of all, unfathomable.

The future can be glimpsed,
>   > but it cannot be known.

?

Who says reality is as we perceive it?

Who says there's nothing else?

>Who says there is?

Who runs your life?

>Do you?

Who tells us right from wrong?

>Do we agree?

>>Or do we obey?

Who says I can't leave, or that I have to?

>Who says I must stay?

Who tells me who I am?

>What I am?

>>Do I know?

Who says I must pay to stay alive?

>That I am indebted simply for living?

Who tells me where I sit in the grand scheme?

>Who knows me better than me?

?

    Do I simply listen?

        Or do I think for myself?

REFLECTIONS

Sentient Beings, Slipper Soldiers
Vestiges of a time past and a future unimagined
Calliope music comes gleaming through the clouds;
It's hard to see what you can't understand.

Shadow Men, Rolling Boulders
Allusions to a story well-told and a life wrongly lived.
Dancers take the livestock and sweep into the stars;
It's easy to believe what you already know.

Pouring Rain, Rising Crops
Almighty cogs in the revolving wheel of life.
Rivers pour down mountains and run into cities;
It's easy to understand the things you see.

Titillating Occultists, Natural Philosophers
Looking glasses fine-tuned to the unknown
and witnesses to God.
We are all born into a dream and wake up with tenure in reality;
It's hard to know what you do not believe.

DREAMING OF NIRVANA

Is it madness to believe that none of this is real?
All these sights that I see, all these emotions I feel...

Am I a fool to think reality is only a fine illusion?
That my perception has fallen between the crosshairs of delusion...

That our world is but a mirage spurned by weary souls who've long since wandered off the road less traveled?
They say reality is ultimately forged in the mind, and when this is realized, the senses become unraveled...

If I've created you, then who are you to me?
A piece of myself, maybe...

What is heaven anyway, and can't I find it here?
It is the light I see, looking up from the nadir...

What must I do to get there, or is it prearranged?
A mind transfigured is a destiny changed...

Can I work off my karma, or is eternal rebirth my demise?
With every enlightened soul, another universe dies...

Is damnation the end of my misled ambition?
Hell, after all, is mindless repetition...

Must I work in heaven, or will it be my reward on that day?
At home, with the tribulations of incarnation far away...

DREAMING OF NIRVANA

> Dreaming of nirvana in endless night, I toss off the down-blankets of maya and rest my head on the pillow of brahmavidya...
> So that when I wake, I may do so in paradise?

SYNCH

Synchronicity, Synchronicity

—the breath of miracles and the claim of madmen.

Synchronicity

—dazzling in occult wonder, mysterious and fatalistic.

Synchronicity

—the delight of the common man & bane of the ignorant.

Synchronicity

—the foothold of religion and the backbone of destiny.

Synchronicity

—the waking life of dreams & explanative of nightmares.

Synchronicity

—and its vibrations, the vibrations of all—
                           the rise and the fall—
                           that gentle tenor—
                  the heartbeat of the universe—
                        blissful and eternal—
                              synch—
always in time, or rather, abiding by its' charming illusion.

SYNCH

Synchronicity

—so outré and yet so ordinary.

Unus Mundus

—synchrony vast and grand—
              through your gentle embrace—

may I dance merrily down the path of enlightenment.

THE LOOKING GLASS

Oh what else is there to do

But gaze up at the azure blue?

A sky made so bright

By the most heavenly light.

Where the clouds so serene,

So pure and white and clean,

Dance across its sempiternal face

As ceaseless and unbroken as empty space.

Look here at this timeless allure,

This infinite grace, perception's door.

What you see has always been,

Through ages past and time again.

For millions of years our Earth has turned,

While all of mankind has watched and learned

To wonder and question ourselves and our world

Since the first thoughts in human minds swirled.

THE LOOKING GLASS

We've grown and evolved:

Many queries have been answered,

many problems solved

Cities and cultures have been built and through war,

Torn to the ground.

Yet we profess, "to morality we are bound."

To gods and philosophies, we give our oath,

Yet all the books others write, we send up in smoke.

A shame it is to see

All these things let be;

For each generation that lives and dies

Sees our world through different eyes.

And this then begs the question,

If I may dare to mention:

Are we educated monkeys,

Or self-aware man?

The truth of this is unknown, though one thing is sure:

To the whole of the universe,

THE LOOKING GLASS

> We are an infinitesimal blur.
>
> Yet, despite our shortcomings as lords of the Earth,
>
> We far surpass our ancestors with every new birth.
>
> Our technologies and systems advance every day,
>
> Our –ology's and creeds, they pave the way
>
> For a future so grand we can't even imagine—
>
> It's either that, it seems, or sinful oblivion.
>
> But for today, all we can do is admire
>
> The things that man has thought and acquired
>
> Through intelligent design or even luck,
>
> All as a side effect of looking up.

WEATHER-MAN

Optimism is the blue-sky alternative to darkness;

cynicism always yields to stormy weather;

pessimism is monsoon season year-round

—and it is eternally sunny to the idealist.

A realist accepts conditions as they are;

a narcissist believes the weather is tailor-made for them;

a nihilist believes weather doesn't really exist;

a skeptic's sky is always obscured by clouds

—and the hedonist finds himself sunburnt year-round.

What's it look like outside your window?

THE WINDOW

    Clouds drift, the Earth turns, Time passes, and I stay.

    I turn, Time drifts, Earth stays, and the Clouds pass.

    Time turns, Earth passes, I drift, and the Clouds stay.

    Earth drifts, the Clouds turn, Time stays, and I pass.

THE SEVEN DEADLY SINS

Death thwarts all those passions which are averse to illumination—you cannot get over on God.

When a prideful man dies, he takes not with him his acclaim, only his pride.

When a greedy man dies, he takes not with him his wealth, only his greed.

When a lustful man dies, he takes not with him his conquest, only his lust.

When an angry man dies, he takes not with him the rotten fruits of his revenge, only his anger.

When a gluttonous man dies, he takes not with him his distention, only his gluttony.

When an envious man dies, he takes not with him those objects he desires, only his envy.

When a lazy man dies, he takes not with him his respite, only his laziness.

However, when an enlightened man dies, he takes not with him the empty pleasures of the world, only his enlightenment.

THE POSTER

I live beneath the bodies of dead men,
Vested in a search to bare their innermost ponderings
—Years past—
Known only to themselves and the universe—
The consciousness that dwells within all.
It is a quest for self-discovery
With a side effect of resurrection.

SO'HAM ASMI, UNUS MUNDUS

As existence gives birth to being, being substantiates knowledge.
As knowledge is the root of all conscious thought, so grow the feelings of sensory experience.

—Simultaneously—

As sensory experience gives birth to thought, thought substantiates knowledge.
As knowledge is the root of all being, so grows existence.

BEN

C'mon everybody, let's get high!

We'll run to the stars with
        reckless abandon.

We'll marry the wind
        and divorce the Earth.

We'll make love to the sun in the light of day
    and by midnight's crescent, dance to please the gods.

Let's get drunk on freedom
        and inebriated by sacrifice.

Let's laugh at our follies
        and toast to our inadequacies.

Let's love, really love—
        love by letting go.

Let's live and let live—
        love and let love.

Let's give rest to everything we've ever known,
        close our eyes and spin around twice—

To fall into the arms of fate,
        floating on the wings of chance.

THE MUSIC SHOPPE

Up here in mid-air suspension,

Second-floor illumination—

Rows and rows of plastic cases

Rise up out of wood-floor panels

Like pyramidic ridges on the sea floor.

I am here above;

Below, life abounds—

Shuffling about,

Minds meandering,

Eyes all browsing the multitudes.

Sounds ring out from sources uncertain:

Rhythmic rocking—synchronous pounding—

Smooth jazz or some new-age Indie shit—

Don't you know it's all the same to me?

They're really just sounds—sprung from the womb of silence.

THE MUSIC SHOPPE

> Outside, the world passes by,
>
> Unaware of the inside—
>
> But it all begins inside.
>
> The doors open and we spill out,
>
> Sounds in tow—perception soon to follow.

PLAY ME SOMETHING BLUE

Play me something dark and low.

Play me something soft and full of smiles and tears.

Play me something that hides behind wisps of hair

and seeps from your eyes flashes at a time.

Play me something deep that makes me think and forget.

Play me something high, so that I may be so.

Play me something mellow that yearns

and waits for someone to listen.

Play me something that I remember

yet have never heard before.

Play me something that sounds like both love and hate,

something that is both joy and pain, tender and cruel.

Play me something that allows me to step

in-between the lines for a time,

out of myself, and into you.

I'll listen.

ANOTHER SHORT POEM ABOUT WORDS

The peculiar sound of words the first time they are spoken
fall upon my ears as they escape past unsteady lips
and linger, quiveringly, on the tongue. They rush toward
me as they brush up against air for the first time and are
free, released from the undulations of the uncertain
mind that bore them. With such poise are they spoken,
with such striking resolve do they fly.
Why is it that we attend to the silence that follows
with such grave intent,
as if we should expect it to also speak?
For silence is eternal,
and words are but fleeting gasps of the breath of life.

OLD STOMPING GROUNDS

>Shadows waltz amongst my memories hence:
>
>Little mirages that waver with the sunlight,
>
>Figures filtering time in their eyes,
>
>Turning back the years with a glance.
>
>Feelings echoed by the landscape,
>
>Walking through the space within a dream.
>
>A feat of double exposure;
>
>A fleeting glimpse of the past.

SOME NIGHTS

Some nights, I think of you.

Some nights when the music is soft and the lights are low,
memories of you dance in my mind.

Some nights, when I am alone, I hear your voice.

Some nights, when I am lonely, I see your face—
the gentle radiance in your eyes ignites an old,
dim flame in my soul.

Some nights I hear your warm laugh,
glimpse your tender smile.

Some nights I can touch you once more
and feel the emotion swell in my heart.

Some nights, for only a moment, I can remember
how we were for all those nights so long ago.

Some nights, I think of love.

LOVE IS

Love is…

    your warm kiss on a cold night.

Love is a soft touch, a swift punch.

Love is silence, not words.

Love isn't a ring, it is a reason.

Love isn't found in the heart, but in the eyes.

Love is a mother's unmuffled cry.

Love isn't the last laugh, it is the first tear.

Love is the knock at the door when you least expect it.

It is the last drop at the bottom of the bottle;
                    the shirt off my back.

Love is the road less traveled; it is full of thorns,
                  briars,
                  & felled trees.

It is not well trodden.

It is muddy, and the sky is dark

        …but love is light.

LOVE IS

    It is morning's gentle glow at the dawn of each new day.

    Love is unescapable—not by dreams nor wishes,

                            thought nor power.

    Love is having nothing and wanting nothing.

    Love is holding everything in your arms.

    Love is not of the mind.

    It cannot be touched, only felt—

    In presence,

        in absence,

             in life,

             and in death.

    Love is that unspoken omission between you and the universe.

    That little smile that no one else understands.

YOU HAVEN'T LOVED…

You haven't loved until you have lost.

You haven't lived until you have felt a part of you die.

A WOMAN WALKED INTO THE OCEAN

A woman walked into the ocean in a red ball gown…

And uncertainty was all she found.

All the lies and all the fights

Had led to nothing more than early respite.

She'd said to him that evening past,

"You come first, and I, last.

Admit it, that I am right,

Or I will end it all tonight!"

He raised his voice, his anger strong,

"Have you the audacity to call me wrong?

Should this be the day you leave,

No man on Earth would rightly grieve!"

Out from the hall and the courtyard she fled,

Across the moonlit sand her bare feet tread.

She alighted the tide with poise and grace

As a single, salty tear ran down her face—

A WOMAN WALKED INTO THE OCEAN

>To meet the wave for which it was bound
>
>And her soles at once left the earthly ground.
>
>Her body turned toward the deep,
>
>The Almighty God she did entreat;
>
>"The only fate worse than this
>
>Is forever in his kiss.
>
>Running away would not suffice,
>
>If only death were paradise…"

THE LIGHT

> The Light quickens in those who are hopeful and burns bright in those who believe.
>
> The Light is inextinguishable, even by the strongest wind, the largest flood, or the most barren earth.
>
> The Light hangs on like an eternally dying ember cloaked by ash in the soul of those whose flame has dimmed.
>
> The Light is the means by which we live and are alive— that which we could not be without.
>
> Within the reaches of the Light, no dark can remain— only the shadows of our fears, the illusion of our misfortune, and the reflection of ourselves.
>
> —And the Light caresses every corner of the universe.
>
> Within the Light is concealed the Truth, and although it may be hard to discern,
>
> Although the pain of perseverance may stun the senses and goad the doubts,
>
> Once the Light of Truth has been seen, the viewer will never see anything other.
>
> For by then, his mortal eyes will have been destroyed—

THE LIGHT

—So that the Light is the last thing he will ever behold.

Illumination is not for the faint of heart.

It is not for those who think,

it is the reward of those who know.

It is not for those whose identity hangs in the balance,

it is the life's work of those who believe in what they cannot yet see.

It is not for those who are the sum of their desires

—it is for those who create their own destinies.

PROSE

PROMETHEUS' FOLLY

The sky at dawn is pink with dew and alive with the sounds of the planets in the morning. I can see every star as it dips below the horizon and the first timid rays of sunlight as they creep above the hills. Tendrils of fern and flower unfurl as the casimi moon yields to the bright glow of day. The grass at my feet, healthy and high, glistens as the new light reflects off last night's rain. A field mouse clings to a blade and quenches his almighty thirst. Broad leaves in the towering trees above shiver as a cool wind rocks their branches. It blows my hair and stirs the water of the nearby stream, forming tiny little whitecaps in the flowing current. The water, clear and pure, runs over smooth, polished river rocks and little twigs sail along into the forest deep. The water sings as it flows along, gurgling and bubbling, rejoicing in its freedom. I dip my head down and take a drink. The liquid is cold and fresh and tastes like life itself. A sound in the distance causes me to startle. I clutch my infant to my breast and turn to see my husband coming quickly down into the clearing. He is not alone. In his hand he holds a piece of the sun, clinging to the end of a stick, burning fiercely, tremendously. Awed and trembling I kneel, prostrate upon the earth in reverence to the thing—that mighty power, God itself.

PROMETHEUS' FOLLY

Heaven came to Earth in this way, escorted by a mere mortal, blazing power in the trifling hands of early man. All civilizations smiled on that primeval day long ago, before time itself, and way up in the recesses of ether and ichor, looking down upon this quaint little Eden and the man who accidentally happened upon a chance to possess the divine, the whole of the pantheon, for the future, cried.

THE MIRROR

Peek behind the round of a grassy knoll and feast your eyes on a world of magic; a world of premonitions and foreknowledge, history and mystery. A haze of disbelief cloaks this ethereal world, paired with devotion so strong it can be made to shake the foundations of the earth it is built upon. It is a puny little biome inhabited by the strangest of creatures—those with both the power to heal and hurt, bear and kill, love and hate. It is a world with no known equal, both doomed and destined.

Its natives are extreme beings. They feel the most alive when they are either creating life or when they are ending it. Sex and war are their most romanticized institutions, made ever more enticing by the egregious hand of avarice. Avarice is a malignant growth in the very heart of their race, fueled by cancerous greed. They buy and sell their bodies and souls and reduce their sentience to mere dollar signs. Their worth is determined by their desirability, a bar set unattainably high and continually augmented so that it lies forever just beyond their means. They prostitute themselves and pillage the less fortunate in order to afford their livelihood. They build temples to secularity and wage war for the sake of freedom. They are doomed to die, yet helplessly hope.

At the dawn of each new day, sunlight oozes out over the horizon like blood from shallow wounds and they rise, determined to carry out their fickle little lives with as few casualties as possible.

THE MIRROR

They remember the trials of yesteryear and forget about yesterday. They plan for the future and disregard the fact that they are never guaranteed a tomorrow. They eat and drink, sin and pray, live and die.

And here I stand, naked, stumbling over words in an attempt to describe them. They are meaningless, empty, broken words lamenting the plight of a meaningless, empty, broken people. They and their words are unsustainable—they cannot stand alone, and they cannot be pieced together. They cry, they scream, they long and they reach out, unavailed. Theirs are sounds, mere sounds—syllables that try so hard to fill the void and fail every time.

They are us, and we are them. Their follies are familiar, their triumphs our own. We can identify with their every wish and abide by their every failure. We see them as erring and infallible, yet perfectly flawed at the same time. We idolize their accomplishments and despise their shortcomings. We watch with bated breath as they stumble and clutch our hearts when they fall.

As we traverse the fated highlands of our reality, confined to the planes of our finite perception, we carry with us their most sublime concentrations of mind. We are born with the entirety of their execrable history heavy upon our backs and die having added to it only our own.

THE MIRROR

For 200,000 years they have struggled and mourned, and for 200,000 more, it seems, we will carry on their tradition of suffering. They have not yet dipped their toes into the respite of objectivity, and as a result, nor have we. The most sanguine of anthropologists believe that it is only a matter of time before one of them casts their eyes upon the waters and sees there the reflection of change, and until that day, we will be waiting.

COEXIST

As humans we are sadistic, murderous, and suicidal. We are born into a world we have proven time and time again to possess an innate hatred for. We have no respect for the condition of the planet that begot us, no sense of wonder surrounding the miracle of life, no inclination to wonder, to appreciate, or to give rather than take. We consider our species superior for such trivial reasons without regard to the complexity, antiquity, or necessity of the rest of the life on this Earth. It is in this way that language hinders rather than empowers. It is the inability to communicate that excuses us from moral accountability, empathy, and understanding. We seem to have adopted an instinct of not only disregarding the pain and suffering of our fellow beings, but the penchant to inflict it consciously, willingly, and repeatedly. Do we act in this manner out of necessity, or is it greed? Is it alternatives we lack, or is it the ability to feel? Why is a species so educated, so self-aware, and so technologically advanced so full of hate? So ignorant? So fond of our ignorance? We consider ourselves lords of the Earth because in the eyes of the past, we have won. Man has battled and struggled against everything in his world since the dawn of his creation—and in time, he has conquered. At the very end of a long and weary path of destruction, he has cemented his lonely existence.

The principle of co-existence seems to be a virtue we lack on a grandiose scale, for man is at war with the very essence of his being.

COEXIST

We have come so far as to kill, maim and transpose our Earth, only allowing the continuation of life if it satisfies or pleases us—if it contributes to the advancement of our backward lifestyle, to the evolution of a species that honors death when for a cause deemed expedient or profitable. Successes, it seems, are enumerated by degrees of separation between our natural world and the world we have manufactured to suit our crude, unnatural desire to assert dominance over each other, to put one another down in order to uplift ourselves, to restrict or exterminate life in order for us to live in luxury. In light of our actions, it seems the very fabric of our society is synthetic, while the death around us is very much real. For as long as we continue to live here on this sorrowful star, the very earth around us will continue to weep for our injustices and suffer because of our missteps. We do not see, we do not hear, we do not feel—and as our Mother slowly dies, we continue to administer the poison. It is only after we have passed the point of redemption that we will truly realize we were wrong; only after we have dug ourselves a hole so deep we cannot escape it will we begin to try. Only after we seek to change will we realize that we cannot. It is only then that we will truly see, only then that we will truly understand the living hell that we have unleashed upon ourselves and our children. It is then that the hunter will become the hunted, the oppressor will become the oppressed, and the killer—the killer will be killed.

NIGHT TERRORS

Every evening when the sun goes down, I sweat. I sweat so much it soaks my scalp and runs down my face and my neck and my back—it drips down my ankles and pools in my boots.

A shock of cold like lightning bolts through me when I think about sleep, and a high voltage short through my veins wakes me in terror when I hear the slightest sound—along with that jerk of sudden motion, that dizzying feeling when instinct takes over and the body moves before the brain is awake enough to comprehend its action. A squirrel scampering across a rustling bed of leaves and twigs is more than enough to make a man grab his rifle, especially a man as scared as me—

—as scared as anyone who's been out in the snow, in the rain, in the oppressive heat packing thirty pounds of gear and blindly fighting an enemy as fearsome and elusive as the devil himself.

You can't make it without sleep. God knows I've tried. The paranoia, the restlessness, and the fear are only greater the longer you go knowing the inevitable—that sometime today or tomorrow or the next day you'll have to lay down your weary, pounding, ravaged head and close your battle-scarred eyes. It's worse knowing the human necessity that was once respite is now nothing but a catch-22—and your worst nightmare. Go without and madness will drive you to an early grave; cave to the sandman's insidious urgings and death may kiss you sweetly in the midst of a dream—and you'll never hear the bullet.

Forget about everything you once knew—sleep in war bears little resemblance to the reveries you remember

NIGHT TERRORS

from back in the world. In war, when waking life itself is a nightmare, sleep is hardly reprieve. Here, dreams cannot exist in any form—for any trace of them is drowned out by the screams of the wounded and crushed by the bodies of the fallen.

You can forget entirely about the notion of comfort—for that is just another seven-letter word here. Even the memories of stuffed mattresses and feather pillows, teddy bears and down comforters are hard to recall, if only due to the fact that the idea that were once real is so very hard to believe. Those things to us are now no more than mere dreams, they're fantasies—and only entertained by the man whose goal it is to drive himself sick with desire. The only pillow you get here is your buddy's twitching side, the only mattress the hard ground, infected by a dampness that seeps into the depths of your bones and stays with you the whole day through, sapping your strength and rotting your brain from the inside out. The only teddy bears you get in a trench or a foxhole are the snakes and rats with whom you share it, and the only cover you are allowed is that of darkness, of night—and it sweeps in fast and low like a heavy round and cloaks the whole area in a blanket of fear.

Night is the common enemy of every soldier—hero and coward alike. You cannot persuade the darkness with a billy-club or strike it down with a sword. You can't pierce the veil of night with a bayonet or blow those formless sounds to smithereens with a grenade—and worst of all, the terrors that come in the shape of nightmares cannot be gunned down or exploded. These

NIGHT TERRORS

here are the most vicious horrors of war—the battles that don't end with the armistice—the wounds that never heal; evidence of the intimate exchange that takes place within the midst of every conflict, in which the war claims your innocence and you carry a part of it home in your heart, filling the empty space where there was once a piece of yourself you've since left behind.

While merciless sleep holds the body in chains, your very sanity fights a nightly battle against the ravages of war, where the moral anguish, the incomprehensible brutality, the savage acts stir again to waltz amongst your memories. They are the threats you cannot see nor hear, the enemies that inflict wounds that cannot be treated—neither sewed up nor sawed off.

They say in hell there will be wailing and gnashing of teeth. I hear it nightly. That hell they speak of is not only a place evil men go after death parts them from this wretched life, it can be found alive and well inside my mind, and it will abide there in irrevocable asylum until the day I die. You see, these malingering vestiges stay alive long after the fighting has ended; for they feed like parasites on the fear, the fear that fears itself.

A CURT RANT ABOUT THE EVILS OF THE WORLD

Rome was hardly built in a day, but its fall was swift due to moral decay.

We stand on a precipice at the edge of a cliff called the future, pushed tirelessly on by the drive of the past.

With progress coming in leaps and bounds, exponentially improving in the blink of an eye, the present seems to slip away before it is even present.

Now is more elusive than ever.

We can treat almost all sickness, and yet we routinely drum up ways to kill one another in increasingly unique and barbaric ways.

We can make our fruit brighter, our cows fatter, and our soil richer, yet millions starve.

We are technically free but realistically bound.

We are subjectively visionary but objectively blind.

Greed and hatred, cruelty and deception continue to haunt our 'civilized world'.

We are the most educated generation ever to live, but by far the most ignorant.

A CURT RANT ABOUT THE EVILS OF THE WORLD

We can build up a virtual world with the swipe of a finger, but we consciously allow the real one around us to disintegrate.

We have the most potential but the least ability.

We have all the tools but no motivation.

To me, it seems, the stumbling block of modern man is the screen he has pulled down over his own eyes.

Used improperly, this technology does no more than hide reality behind a shade of our own creation.

Laziness, impatience, inanity, hypersensitivity, overstimulation—these are but mere side effects of a far more sinister and serious affliction.

We have children that do not listen and parents that refuse to grow up.

We have governments that refuse to be ruled and populations who refuse to rule themselves.

We have an Earth that is frying itself from the inside out.

Need I go on?

With such dire and pervasive afflictions impacting the lives of each and every one of us, you would think we would join together to combat those troublesome forces.

You would be wrong.

A CURT RANT ABOUT THE EVILS OF THE WORLD

> For the first time in human history, we have access to every question that man has ever carried upon his breast in the palm of our hands.
>
> We have the uninhibited means to explore the secrets of existence and discover the similarities we share in order to make peace with our fellow man, but instead we use this priceless resource to investigate the trivial, the mundane, the menial, the artificial, and the superficial.
>
> We're walking around with little Pandora's Boxes in our pockets and we use them to entertain—and even worse—to control, to manipulate, and to bully one another.
>
> Imagine the limitless power that we willingly surrender to those who are smart enough to look above the screens? But alas, few do—and few care—because in this new age of artificial intelligence and mass stupidity, who the hell even thinks anymore?

ESOTERIC MUSINGS OF A DAY LABORER

It has occurred to me of late that Earth is nothing but a cosmic nursery school for spiritual beings—for the lot of us are as destructive and endearing as children. We are, on the whole, beings who will pound the very life out of one another, fight mercilessly over the pettiest of slights, become bitter enemies for a time, and then forget it all when the wind changes course. We commit the same follies time and time again and go on expecting a different result. We yearn so passionately for greener pastures that we allow the ones at home to wither, brown, and die. We are capable of great feats and yet do not realize our true power. We believe in fairytales and dream big dreams. We cry and laugh, we grow angry and pout, we are silly and serious, contemplative and thoughtless, ingenious and dull. We are indiscriminately generous and yet as selfish as can be. We are egocentric, skeptical, arrogant, and yet, beguiled by the beauty and wonder of this world. We are truly remarkable beings. We fall down and get back up, are knocked over and stand again our whole lives through—after all, there is no will more indominable than that of a child.

However, there seems to be a ubiquitous and disquieting factor that characterizes the whole of human experience—and the older we get, the more it seems to present itself. We seem to be afflicted by a deep and fundamental loneliness. It is as if the world goes by and we are alone on an island, stranded in the middle of the sea of serendipity. We forget we have in our power free

ESOTERIC MUSINGS OF A DAY LABORER

will; the law of attraction. We forget that loneliness is but an illusion. We forget that no matter how hard we try we can never separate ourselves from one another—the ones we love nor the ones we hate—because, really, we are all one, together.

In order for our spiritual bodies to grow, we must be nourished by the waters of enlightenment. In order to rise above our station in this life and refuse to be such worldly men, life itself must be seen as a dynamic process, or we and everything else are simply spinning free in entropy: lost without a cause, a way, or a befitting idea. We must open our embryonic minds to those notions we cannot perceive, those ideas not our own, and the unity and oneness that lies at the heart of all things. There is so much more between heaven and hell than any man could ever tell, and the man who thinks he knows it well is the most ignorant of all.

As spiritual beings temporarily inhabiting the world of matter, we are essentially likened to a fish out of water or a bird of flight trapped in a cage. We are merely stewards of this world, not rulers of it as we dare to imagine. Any attempt to preserve and accumulate material wealth—or 'possessions', as you may call them—is not only vain but pathetic.

ESOTERIC MUSINGS OF A DAY LABORER

> The only part of this world that we take from it on the event of our passing is the karma we have accrued in our spiritual bankbooks—therefore the rich man on his deathbed is just about as lucky as the assassin who boards the Stygian ferry with a license to kill.

THE SEA

We each move through life as if we know where we are going, as if we have some trajectory and are gliding effortlessly along one seamless straight line that bridges birth to death. In reality, however, we are floating—bobbing up and down in an endless sea, and we die with the same uncertainty with which we were born. There are certain paths we are expected to follow, certain directions we hope to take, brief flashes of inspiration that make possible a mere moment of clarity, a glimpse of what may seem like truth, but really, it is only an illusion—a wave, a mirage, a ship we seek to board, a vessel we yearn to cling to in hopes that we will reach heaven in its wake. But it is all in vain. Not one of us knows where he will end up, no matter how self-assured or critically acclaimed he may be. We face life with such force and intensity and forget that when you strike out against the ocean, it merely moves away, unaffected.

However powerless we may feel, it is only the tip of the iceberg. We must keep searching for the truth with every breath, lashing out for a handhold on reality. We must keep our heads above the waterline of despair and entropy, for if we sink below in forfeit, we will surely drown, caught in the tide of our own misgivings. This apparent madness encompasses all and everything, and despite what we may think we know, there is no more certainty guaranteed in life than there is given to a man adrift at sea.

A MUSING

All these picturesque glimpses of life are but unsubstantiated dreams that we carve for ourselves out of a large, dull, and featureless rock unaffected by the happenstance and circumstance of reality. They are but reactionary mechanisms built up to slake the fears of sentient minds living in entropy. Tomorrow is but a guess, today is yesterday's wish, and the present moment slides by as unnoticed as a single breath. Dwell we must on the stuff of dreams, or else we may never live. We walk blindly along the very edge of the straight and narrow and balance precariously on the precipice of fate. Destined are we to choose the life we imagine for ourselves, but doomed we are to fail.

MADNESS

A little bit of madness laps at the shores of the minds of those for whom life is a dream and reality is a nightmare.

A little bit of sanity finds a foothold in the mountains of fear, cloaked by a heavy fog of doubt.

It is not at leisure that one forgets the murky past they have traversed, nor do they take great pleasure in remembering.

On the misty flats drift the souls of those burdened with sight beyond that which their eyes can provide and their minds can perceive.

To and fro, they wander in the frozen night, lost without direction in the soundless abyss.

Trapped between two worlds, they whisper and pray, a resident of neither, a stranger to both.

A CONTEMPLATION

In the great myriad of human misconception, there exists a significant yet minute hope imbedded within all of us that one day we might find true love. Yet it ensues, that for those who need it most, liberation comes too late.

Shall it be called divine intervention that a select few still manage to find it?

Or is it so that in the vastness of our minds we can manage to conjure up the absurd reality that we will ever find it at all?

We humans look at life so intently and try so desperately to deduct meaning from it that in doing so, it loses any meaning it ever had.

The vague and relative symbolism with which we cloak our world detracts from its essence insomuch as it assuages our consciences.

When we analyze our surroundings with such pinpoint accuracy and attempt to ascribe status to every crack and crevice and assign every molecule as either "this" or "that", the beauty and singularity of existence fades away.

Reality is not a textbook, in which the elements of our lives are meant to be dissected and slid under the microscope of subjectivity for analysis.

Nor is reality a *SparkNotes* reader, in which snippets of experience are tied together by coincidence and the human need for logic and patterns and then forced to perform ugly, unnatural rituals year after year as each new generation stands in awe of those who interpreted them either as cultural totems or personal talismans.

We have a very unfortunate tendency to look past what we are looking at to find what we are looking for.

A flashing green light is not always a beacon, nor must a raven ignite such fear—and I've yet to see bad luck seep from the fissures of a broken mirror.

Delineating the facts of life may bring us knowledge, but rarely does it bring us peace.

Knowing things, albeit great, can only get us so far, and there are some times when we must admit that a cigar is just a cigar.

THE POSSIBLE IMPOSSIBILITY

In order to truly *UNDERSTAND*, one must first release all that those before him have claimed to have understood—cultures, religions, ethos, pathos, and all precedents impartially—and live by what he feels is right and correct. He must live by the limitations of his own imagination and listen to the teaching of his own soul—all in a state of physical, mental, and emotional *COMFORT*.

I wonder how Buddha felt?

—Buddha felt like...*YOU*!

—When you release all inhibitions and fears and in turn stand naked before God—ourselves—what is one and all—the Mind—just in time for Kairos!—The supreme moment, *NOW*!

Wait a moment before passing your judgement: your practical reasoning—technicalities, technicalities—the this or that, the how or why such actions cannot be achieved in *PRACTICAL APPLICATION*.

In a world of practicality, all humanity seems a tad overdue—in the midst of all our marvelous, colorful, magnificent hang-ups—for a bit of impracticality. Oh, our glorious attachments! Those wonderfully weeping for love and lust, greed and capitalist gallantry, anger and

THE POSSIBLE IMPOSSIBILITY

regrets—the great clot—the cerebral noise converging upon, suffocating and choking the unsuspecting host until in a single moment, death. In a single moment, fear. In a single moment, freedom. In a single moment, the eternal moment, *YOU—US—I—THEM—ALL*. Blooming like the lotus, budding as the blossoms do in spring, spilling out like water over a cliff and falling out into—*NOTHING—EVERYTHING—ETERNITY*—and radiating *TOTAL LOVE* and *UNDERSTANDING*.

Finding peace in self—and self in all—the most unlikely reality proclaims the truth—traveling in spectacular undulations as pure as spirit and baptized in *ABIDING PEACE*.

www.ingramcontent.com/pod-product-compliance
Lightning Source LLC
Chambersburg PA
CBHW020545080526
44583CB00013B/995